NSPCC happy Kids

CHILD CARE GUIDES

Sleeping Through the Night

by

Faye Corlett

EGMONT WORLD

"The National Society for the Prevention of Cruelty to Children (NSPCC) has a vision – a society where all children are loved, valued and able to fulfil their potential. The NSPCC is pleased to work with Egmont World Limited on the development of this series of child care guides. We believe that they will help parents and carers better understand children's and babies' needs."

Jim Harding, Chief Executive, NSPCC.

Designer: Dave Murray
Illustrator: John Haslam
Editor: Stephanie Sloan
Cover designer: Craig Cameron
Front cover photograph supplied by Stockbyte

The NSPCC Happy Kids logo and Happy Kids characters:
TM & © NSPCC 2000. Licensed by CPL
NSPCC Registered Charity Number: 216401

Published in Great Britain in 2000 by Egmont World,
an imprint of Egmont Children's Books Limited,
239 Kensington High Street, London, W8 6SA.
Printed in Italy. Reprinted 2001.

ISBN 0 7498 4775 1

A catalogue record for this book is available
from the British Library.

Sleeping through the night

by Faye Corlett

Contents

Introduction

Sleep is a topic close to most parents' hearts – so take comfort in the fact that you are not alone! Sleep deprivation can be very debilitating, leaving you questioning your ability to cope. This book offers you practical solutions and reassurance. It explains your baby's sleep patterns and gives advice that allows both you and your baby to get a good night's sleep.

Note:
When referrring to the child, we have alternated the use of he and she throughout the book.

CHAPTER 1

Sleep – your baby and you

Think of a baby, a new-born baby, and nine times out of ten the image that comes to mind is that of a soundly-sleeping infant, lying all cosy, warm and innocent in his cot watched over by a favourite teddy bear. Now think about the amount of time and effort it probably took his mum or dad to get him off to sleep. They might have got up to tend to his cries many times that night, leaving either one or both of them red-eyed and exhausted.

The question most parents are asked after "How's the baby?", is "Is he sleeping through the night yet?" And in those first few hectic, chaotic months of having a new baby in the house, sleep will be a topic close to most parents' hearts. Will the baby ever stop waking five times a night? Will he ever sleep through? Please, please, please, when are we going to be able to get some sleep?

If you are feeling tired out and demoralised from trying to soothe your baby to sleep, time and time again, take comfort in the fact that you are not alone. Babies are not born with an in-depth knowledge about the different times of day. They're not aware that adults have general routines and certain times for having a meal or going to bed. They certainly have no preconception about what night-time is and that night-time is when we prefer to get our sleep. All baby will have on his mind in the first months is making sure his stomach is constantly filled with milk, and he won't mind if he has to wake you at 2am every morning to do this, and then again in another couple of hours!

If you're prepared not to get too much in the way of uninterrupted sleep in baby's first three months, you won't be disappointed. The majority of babies are going to wake once or more each night during this time. 75% of babies are sleeping through by the time they reach six months, so things should improve for you, and soon.

A minority of babies, however, are problem sleepers right through their toddler years. Generally, when a new-born baby is sleeping, nothing, but nothing will disturb him. Dogs barking, noisy parties, he's oblivious to them all. But just like some adults, some babies can be light sleepers, waking at the smallest noise. Others will still wake regularly in the night just for reassurance that you are there. Thankfully, most of these problems can be resolved with a little guidance and perseverance. This book will give you some useful tips for both avoiding and solving sleep problems, and provide information on:

- how a baby's sleep patterns will change;
- how to build up a bedtime routine for you and your baby;
- how to provide an environment in which

baby will want to sleep, and which is safe for sleeping in;

• some common sleep problems, and tips for solving them.

So take heart. It can be very difficult indeed to cope initially on the few hours' sleep you manage to snatch here and there. Have sensible expectations right from the start. And while you are suffering the sleepless nights, there are plenty of things you can do to catch up on your sleep and help you cope.

- Sleep when your baby sleeps if you can.

- Ask a family member or friend to mind your baby for a few hours whilst either you or your partner takes a rest.

- Jointly share the baby's care and getting up to baby during the night with your partner so you both have an opportunity to get some sleep.

You'll soon find, especially as you bond with your baby, that you will begin to understand his behaviour – his different cries, his sleep patterns. All this will help in building up a bedtime routine that will prevent difficult sleeping habits from the start. Then both your baby and you will hopefully get to sleep through the night.

CHAPTER 2

What is sleep?

To understand why your baby wakes, it's very useful to know how your baby sleeps, and how her sleep patterns change as she gets older.

Neither adults, children nor babies sleep continuously from the moment they get into bed to the moment they get up. For everyone, sleep is a continuous cycle of different levels of consciousness; light sleep to deepest sleep, dreaming, waking for a moment and then falling asleep again.

In an adult, a complete cycle of sleep is longer than that of a baby, which means that we wake less in the night. When we do wake, we see that it is still dark, and then go back to sleep. Because babies have a shorter sleep cycle, there is more potential for them to wake during the night.

A lucky few parents will find that their baby seems to sleep right through the night from quite a young age. However, the majority of babies don't have a built-in skill to be able to put themselves back to sleep, which is why they cry on waking, especially in the first few months, for you to come and help them settle.

You should soon be able to recognise your baby's periods of lighter sleep which might announce her waking up. Your baby might stretch or yawn, or start to whimper half-heartedly, uncertain if she wants attention, or just wants to go back to sleep.

Babies are also different from adults in that, whereas we drift off to sleep, babies can plunge into a deep sleep very quickly. They will also sleep wherever they find themselves, even in your arms whilst being fed. This being the case, unless she is a very light sleeper, it is unlikely that your baby's sleep will be at all disturbed by household noises. So there's no need to tiptoe around a slumbering new-born baby. It will even be useful for you if your baby gets used to sleeping through a certain amount of noise. If everyone keeps noise to a minimum and talks in whispers whilst the baby is asleep, there may come a time when she will not sleep unless you do. So let your baby sleep through whatever noise level is usual for your household. Generally, the only things that will wake a new-born baby are hunger or some other internal stimulus, such as feeling hot or cold, or uncomfortable.

Sleep patterns

The amount of sleep babies need does vary. Some sleep for long periods, some only for short. Each baby sleeps for the amount of time her own personal body clock tells her to sleep.

- In the first few weeks, although your baby will probably sleep for up to twenty hours each day, her main priority will be keeping her stomach full, so she will wake frequently to tell you she is hungry. It is during this time that your baby is more likely to wake you in the night. It is also unlikely that she will fall asleep happily unless she feels full and satisfied.

- At three months, your baby will be more wakeful and active during the day. 60% of her sleeping time will now be at night, with daytime sleeps short naps, these gradually becoming shorter still as she gets older. You might notice too that she sleeps at more regular times.

- Between six and twelve months, your baby should be spending much less time asleep during the day. Her night-time sleep pattern should also be much more predictable.

So remember that no parent is ever going to be able to defy the laws of sleeping and make their baby sleep continuously throughout the night. Just like us, they will always wake at some stage. What parents can do is to teach their baby when bedtime is coming, the difference between night-time and daytime, and how to go back to sleep without crying for attention.

CHAPTER 3
Safe sleeping

In the early days, when it is typical to be more anxious about your baby and to feel you need to listen for his every sound, it is natural for you to want to have your new infant in a carrycot in your room. If you want to do this at first, that's just fine. The vital thing to remember is, wherever your baby is going to sleep, you need to provide an environment that your baby will be comfortable in, will want to sleep in, and most importantly, is SAFE for sleeping in. If your baby is cosy, comfortable and not too hot or too cold, it makes sense that he's more likely to sleep for longer periods.

Cots, mattresses and other nursery equipment

Always choose equipment that meets current safety standards. If you are buying second-hand, ensure that the equipment is fit for the purpose and not liable to injure your baby.

• Make sure that the cot mattress fits the cot snugly so that there isn't a gap between cot and mattress where your baby could trap an arm or a leg.

- Don't place anything in the cot in which he could become tangled or that could obstruct his breathing. For this reason, cot bumpers are not recommended. These are padded cot sides that are attached to the inside of the cot with ribbon. Although they may make the cot look cosy, they are a safety hazard. The ribbons could become tangled around your baby. Even more importantly, if your baby moves around his cot, there is a danger that he could either press his head up against a bumper or underneath it.

- Have a low-light night-lamp in baby's room to switch on when seeing to baby during the night. It will help to educate your baby about the difference between night-time and daytime if you can make sure the lighting is kept low at night.

- There's still much debate on the use of dummies with babies. However, if your baby is only allowed a dummy until his milk teeth start to appear, it won't do his mouth any serious damage. In fact, there's agreement amongst dentists that it's better for a baby to suck a dummy rather than a thumb, which can do more damage to his teeth. The truth is that a dummy does help to settle a baby, so using one to comfort your baby may be helpful, especially during the first few months. If your baby won't take to a dummy – some don't – or you'd rather not use one, introduce another special bedtime comforter instead, such as a cuddly toy. Make sure baby always has this with him at bedtime to comfort him when he wakes.

The right temperature

Remember that your baby won't be able to remove his clothes or blankets if he is too hot, or snuggle up for warmth if he is too cold. Extremes of temperature can be another factor in him crying for your attention during the night. So,

- make sure that the temperature in his nursery (or in your room if he is sleeping in a carrycot beside your bed) is kept warm enough for comfort. It's as important that it's not too hot as too cold. Generally, between 16 and 20 degrees centigrade will be right for your baby. It's a good idea to buy a simple strip room temperature guide for a wall in baby's room – most baby stores stock them – so that you can monitor the temperature;

- remember not to overdress your baby at bedtime. Always check that he is warm enough by feeling the back of his neck. At most times of the year, a sleepsuit and a blanket will suffice;

- your baby needs to lose heat from his head and face, so, unless it is very cold, always keep your baby's head uncovered when he is in his cot;

- don't use duvets in your baby's cot until he is at least twelve months old. They retain too much heat;
- never use a hot water bottle or an electric blanket in your baby's cot. There is also a danger that these could scald or burn your baby's delicate skin.

CHAPTER 4

Protecting against cot death

Cot death or Sudden Infant Death Syndrome (SIDS) is a terrifying subject for all parents. SIDS is when a perfectly healthy baby is put down to sleep and, without any reason or warning, is later found to be dead. Thankfully, it is not a common incident, affecting only one in every 800 babies. Unfortunately, nobody knows for certain what are the true causes of SIDS. Whatever they are, they cause the baby to stop breathing. What researchers are sure about, however, are the precautions that parents can take to minimise the risk of SIDS.

The following recommendations are listed in the booklet 'Reduce the risk of cot death', published by the Foundation for the Study of Infant Deaths (FSIDS).

• Place your baby on her back to sleep. The risk of cot death is reduced if babies are not put on the tummy to sleep. Side sleeping is not as safe as sleeping on the back but is much safer than sleeping on the front. Healthy babies placed on their backs are not more likely to choke. Older babies are able to turn over and move around the cot. Put them down on the back but let them find their own sleeping position . The risk of cot death in babies over six months is extremely low.

- Cut out smoking during pregnancy – fathers too. Smoking in pregnancy increases the risk of cot death. It is best not to smoke at all, but the less you smoke, the lower the risk.

- Don't let anyone smoke in the same room as your baby. Babies exposed to cigarettes after birth are also at an increased risk of cot death. It is best if nobody smokes in the house, including visitors. Do not take your baby into smoky places.

- Don't let your baby get too hot (or too cold). Overheating can increase the risk of cot death. Babies can overheat because of too much bedding or clothing, or because the room is too hot. A comfortable room temperature is between 16 and 20 degrees centigrade. It is easier to adjust for the temperature with changes of lightweight blankets.

- Keep baby's head uncovered. Babies whose heads are covered accidentally with bedding are at an increased risk of cot death. To guard against this, always place your baby in her cot in the 'feet to foot' position – this means her feet should be put at the foot of the cot and and the bed made up so that the covers are no higher than the shoulders. This will prevent her wriggling down under the covers. Covers should be securely tucked in so they cannot slip over baby's head.

Can baby sleep in our bed?

All parents are tempted to have their baby in bed with them at some stage. If your baby is getting you up many times in the night, it can seem like a convenient option. You might also want baby near you because you are concerned about her health.

However, research into cot death has indicated that babies seem to be at much lower risk of cot death if they sleep in their own cot where there is less chance of them overheating. For babies sleeping in their parents' bed there is also a danger that they could be unknowingly smothered by their parents either rolling onto them or covering their face with the duvet or covers whilst they sleep.

Although these risks may be minimal, parents should be aware of the possible dangers. That doesn't mean that you shouldn't have your baby in with you for an early morning cuddle, but it's good advice to avoid having baby in bed with you when you are sleeping, especially in the early months.

Remember – to reduce the risk of your baby overheating or suffocating, do not use a pillow or a duvet in your baby's cot until she is at least twelve months old.

You are bound to worry about cot death. All parents do, whether it's their first baby or their fifth. Follow the guidance above to help maintain the safety of your baby. Above all, try to keep the worry in perspective by reminding yourself that cot death only affects a tiny minority of babies and the risks greatly reduce as the months go by. The risk of cot death in babies over six months is extremely low.

CHAPTER 5

A bedtime routine for baby

Getting a bedtime routine going with your baby is a very useful way of helping him to realise when 'sleep time' is approaching, so that he settles down more easily, hopefully to sleep through the night.

Bedtime routines are beneficial to both parents and babies. Babies do respond to a familiar routine. They find it comforting and it helps to make them feel safe and secure, which are exactly the sort of feelings a parent wants to teach at bedtime. A planned routine will help your baby steadily wind down and realise that bedtime is coming. It will then be much easier for you to put him down and should help him to quickly drift off to sleep. Building up a routine will also help him to settle more quickly when the surroundings are unfamiliar, for example, if you are on holiday. It follows too that, on the occasions when you are unable to do the bedtime routine with your baby, you make sure that whoever you have entrusted his care to follows the same routine.

In the first few weeks, the fact that your baby wakes during the night will be mostly down to him keeping his stomach full. Although he may seem to spend a great deal of time asleep, a lot of his sleeping will be done during the day. So don't worry at this stage about getting into a definite routine. These early weeks can be the most tiring for parents. With a baby feeding every three hours or so, even Einstein would find it difficult to solve this problem!

When your baby is between six and nine months, you should start to see more of a pattern developing in when he sleeps and feeds. He will probably be falling asleep at more regular times each day. As his behaviour becomes more predictable, this is the best time to start putting together a bedtime routine. Keep it as simple as possible, so that, no matter how tired you are, it will be quick and easy for you to do each evening.

It makes sense too to start putting baby 'to bed' whenever he drops off to sleep and getting him up when he is awake. Rather than letting him snooze on your lap, if he is always put into his cot when he is feeling sleepy, he will soon come to associate this with going to sleep.

Useful tips

- It's a good idea to start the routine with bathing baby in the early evening. You might think that this will make your baby more wakeful, but just as it does for adults, a warm bath, and soothing attention from you, will relax your baby.

- As you dress your baby for bed after his bath, don't make it a playtime or you will only make him wakeful once again. Talk quietly to him, or even sing to your baby if you've got the voice for it! This will also help to educate your baby that the day is winding down and bedtime is coming.

- When he is dressed ready for bed, take baby to his room, and keep the lights low whilst you give him a bedtime feed. Continue to soothe your baby into bedtime mode by quietly talking to him.

- Finally, put baby down in his cot. Make sure he is cosy and comfortable, but not too warm, with his dummy or special comforter if he needs one. As baby gets older, this can be baby's storytime too. Then, after giving him a goodnight kiss, leave him to go to sleep. Once he begins to realise that bedtime is for sleeping, he should hopefully be happy to go to sleep in this way.

The time of day given to start this routine will depend very much on the individual household – but whatever time you start with, try to keep to it, and to the sequence, as much as you can. Changing the routine or not doing it will only make your baby feel disorientated, and more difficult to settle to sleep as he gets older. Some babies can become so used to an exact routine that parents find they cannot change or vary it, even in the smallest way.

Parents should remember to maintain their 'night-time behaviour' with their baby if he does wake in the night. When you comfort your baby during the night, remember to keep both the light and your voice low, so that baby knows it is still sleeping time.

Some lucky parents can manage to establish a bedtime routine when their baby's sleep pattern becomes more regular. But there are many other parents whose babies will continue to have sleep problems in spite of a bedtime routine.

CHAPTER 6

Crying, but not much sleeping

If, after introducing a bedtime routine with your baby, she is still waking and crying for you during the night, don't blame yourself. You're probably not doing anything wrong, and neither is she. A baby's sleep patterns can be quite puzzling for some parents. It can sometimes happen that a baby who has fitted in with her bedtime routine happily at first and her parents have seen real results in getting her to sleep through, will all of a sudden start to wake and cry in the night once more!

Don't despair. Remember that crying is the only way a baby has of getting your attention, to ask for a cuddle, or to tell you that she is hungry or there is something wrong. She may not even know why she is crying – she just knows that something isn't right and she needs mum or dad to make her feel happy again.

If you still have problems with your baby

waking and crying for you at night, try the following tips just one at a time.

• Your baby may be hungry. In the early months, this is almost certain to be the cause of your baby's tears when more frequent feeds are required throughout the day. As baby gets older, she could be waking at night just because she needs larger feeds.

If you are breastfeeding, you could try feeding more frequently, or for bottle-fed babies, give a few extra millilitres at each feed. You could also try increasing the amount you give for her bedtime feed.

- If you've always fed your baby whenever she cries at night to get her back off to sleep, she might just have got into the habit of crying to bring you running with food! If she takes a bottle or a cup, only offer her water and not milk. You might find she gets bored with crying at night if all she's going to get out of it is a drink of water.

- Give your baby a chance to go back to sleep on her own. Don't go in to see to her at the slightest whimper. This doesn't mean leaving baby to cry it out, or to cry herself back to sleep. But you're not being a bad parent if you teach yourself to wait a couple of minutes before you go into your baby. A few whimpers may be all there is to it, and it could let her go back to sleep without fully waking up. In fact, your efforts to soothe her to sleep could be making her fully awake! However, if your baby's cries are frantic and persistent, this is a sign that something is wrong with baby, and should never be ignored.

- She might just need a cuddle. If you do pick her up, rock her gently and speak to her softly. But keep everything low key. Don't play with your baby and make sure that the lights are kept low so you are still teaching her that different behaviour is expected at night.

- Make sure that your baby isn't too hot or too cold. Especially during a change in the seasons, this is a common cause of a baby feeling uncomfortable at night. Feel the back of your baby's neck to see if it feels sweaty or cold, and decrease or increase her bedding and clothing accordingly. Check the room temperature too. It's just as important that it's not too warm as too cold, and ideally should be kept at a constant 16 to 20 degrees centigrade.

- Perhaps where baby sleeps is too quiet. This might sound strange when we adults normally crave a peaceful atmosphere for sleep. However, life in the womb is quite noisy for a baby with the sound of his mother's loud heartbeat in the background, so introducing a regular, rhythmic sound into her room at night could be comforting for her. Try leaving a radio on low volume or a ticking clock in baby's room.

Even if you are having problems with night waking, do persevere with your baby's bedtime routine. This is important for keeping bad sleeping habits at bay in her later years. Remember too that other parents will be experiencing the same difficulties, and for the majority, things will improve in time.

CHAPTER 7
Other causes of sleeplessness

As a parent, you are bound to feel anxious about the health and well-being of your baby. It is also likely that you will experience, on at least one occasion, being woken in the night by your baby crying because he is feeling ill.

As your baby gets older you will naturally start to recognise his different cries and what they mean. He will have a cry for when he is hungry, for when he needs comfort and nearness from you, or when he wants to tell you that something is wrong. In the previous chapter, we've talked about ways to soothe your baby when he wakes in the night, and tips for helping him to sleep through.

However, if there is ever an occasion when your baby cries during the night, or during the day for that matter, and you either recognise that cry as a cry of pain or you are at all concerned about your baby, *never hesitate to seek advice from your doctor or health visitor.* This advice also applies if nothing at all seems to settle your baby, or he will only settle for a few moments before the crying starts up again. You must also be very wary that something is wrong if your baby seems unusually listless and drowsy, and appears to have difficulty feeding.

Colic

- Younger babies may suffer from colic, a kind of stomach cramp. In diagnosing colic, there are some typical signs to look out for, although some babies may not show any of these signs. Your baby might draw his legs up to his stomach and clench his fists,

together with a crying session, which can turn to screaming, that can be quite prolonged. Colic can be triggered by lots of different things: Excess wind, a tummy ache due to something in mum's milk or the bottle formula, or just the fact that the baby's digestive system is maturing. There is no definite explanation for cause.

- The fact that there is no explanation for the cause of colic also means that it has no cure other than by just comforting and rocking your baby. Parents can take heart in the fact that any colicky attacks will normally stop by the time the baby is three months old. This will be a very distressing time for the baby and for the carers, so keep your sanity by sharing the baby's care with your partner and remembering that it is only a phase in your baby's development – it will pass.

Something more serious

Always contact your doctor if you think that your baby is ill, even if you're not sure what is wrong. Trust your instincts. Even if it turns out that your baby isn't ill, that's fine. Don't be afraid of asking for medical help. If your baby displays any, or a combination, of the following signs, seek help straight away.

- A loss of consciousness.

- A convulsion (fit), or blueness of lips or face.

- A very high temperature. The normal body temperature for a child is between 36 and 37 degrees centigrade (97 to 98.6 degrees Fahrenheit). To take your baby's temperature, first rinse the thermometer in cold water and then shake it with a flick of your wrist. Make sure it has a low reading, then place the mercury bulb end under your baby's armpit and hold it in place for two minutes.

- A temperature, but his hands and feet feel cold and clammy.

- Breathing difficulties, breathing fast or noisy breathing, which may be combined with a hoarse cough.

- Unusually drowsy and hard to wake.

- A rash characterised by red or purple spots that look like bleeding under the skin. This is an especial symptom of meningitis, together with unusual drowsiness, crying in an unusual way and refusing to feed. Test to see if the rash fades or loses colour by pressing the side of a glass firmly against your baby's skin. If the rash doesn't fade, contact your doctor immediately. When meningitis is diagnosed and treated early, the majority of babies and children make a full recovery.

- Persistent vomiting and diarrhoea.
- Crying in an unusual way or for an unusually long time, and seeming to be in a lot of pain.
- Refusing feeds.

Make a note here of the contact numbers for your doctor and health visitor, and keep this book in a safe place so that the numbers are quickly accessible when you need them.

DOCTOR   Telephone number

....

HEALTH VISITOR   Telephone number

....

Thankfully, more often than not, the problems of night crying and a wakeful baby can easily be solved. However, it's important that as parents you know how to recognise the warning signs that something is wrong, so that you can quickly act to ensure the health and safety of your baby.

CHAPTER 8

Sleep problems after six months

By six or seven months, your baby will be on solid food and probably displaying a much more regular pattern of when she likes to sleep and feed. Most babies of this age take only a couple of naps during the daytime, one in the morning, and one in the afternoon, and these may be as short as twenty minutes.

Other significant changes in a baby's behaviour also take place around this age. In the first few months, babies normally fall asleep when they need to, and nothing, apart from hunger or pain, will make them wake, generally not even loud household noises happening all around them. At six months, a baby starts to become able to keep herself awake. She will also be much more interested in and aware of what is happening around her. It then follows that she will only go to sleep if she needs to. So although this is the age when most parents can expect their infant to be happily sleeping through, largely because she doesn't need frequent night feeds, it can also be an age when real sleep problems can start for parents.

Don't leave me!

Babies also become more aware of their carers at this age. In baby's early months, mum and dad are very much seen as the people who respond to her needs when she's hungry or needs changing.

As the baby and her special bond with her parents matures and develops, so will her need to be with mum and dad. She might smile and laugh for other faces who peer into her pram or come round to visit, but she will keep her biggest smile for her parents. Although this is a very rewarding aspect of parenthood, it can also mean that baby is difficult to get to sleep because she doesn't want her parents to leave her at bedtime.

- Mums and dads can help overcome this from the start by introducing their baby to a number of close family members who will also play a major part in baby's care.

- If your baby cries each time you try to leave her room, make sure she doesn't feel completely cut off from you. Leave the night light on low and the nursery door open so that she can still hear sounds that will assure her you haven't gone far. You could also try not leaving her room as soon as you've put her down, but, still with the light on low so she recognises it's sleep time, spend ten minutes quietly tidying up and putting away clothes, so that she can settle knowing that you are still near.

Disturbances to sleep

Now that your baby won't be sleeping as deeply as when she was a new-born, be aware that external noises could stimulate her waking in the night: traffic noise, for example, or the sound of you and your partner turning in yourselves. If you live near a busy main road, there might not be anything you can do about this, other than by fitting double-glazing or moving your baby's nursery to the other side of the house. Do try, however, to keep household noise to a minimum once baby is having her night-time sleep.

Early wakers

Babies generally don't have a morning waking time that suits their parents, either. They wake up when they've had enough sleep, and it's probably true to say that most will go through a stage of waking early in the morning. However, unlike their tired-out parents, they won't go back to sleep until the alarm goes off! At this stage in your baby's development, early waking is associated with a real energy to start the day and see what's happening. If your baby does cry for you early in the morning, try the following to see if you can keep her sleeping, or quiet, for longer.

- Check the nursery curtains to make sure that they keep out the early morning light.
- Leave some safe toys in her cot, such as soft, cuddly toys, the sort she can play with without coming to any harm. You might find that she will amuse herself for a while at least. Alternatively, have her playpen in your room so you can bring her there when she cries for you in the morning. Then she will be safe whilst you have a catch-up snooze, and will probably play happily knowing you are nearby.

All these patterns of behaviour are again only phases in your baby's growth and development. Keep reminding yourself that she will grow out of them in time.

CHAPTER 9
Looking after you

"When we found out I was pregnant, we were thrilled and just couldn't wait for it to happen soon enough. We laughed at everyone asking if we were ready for the night feeds – we thought we'd cope quite happily. Our daughter's now five months old, and the thought of those night feeds isn't so funny any more. It seems as if everything is about getting her off to sleep and catching up on sleep ourselves."

"I don't think it's getting the baby off to sleep that's hard to do, it's getting enough sleep ourselves. It's even worse with two children. You get one off to sleep and then the baby will wake for a feed. You just feel you're acting like a robot – baby crying, get up, settle the baby, snatch 40 winks, baby crying, get up, and on, and on, and on."

If you're already a parent, you'll recognise how these parents feel. A baby's sleep patterns are totally unlikely to fit in with ours. We adults need our sleep and sleep deprivation can be very debilitating for even the strongest among us. Without it, we can be at least grumpy and grouchy. At worst, it can leave us questioning our ability to cope with normal, everyday things. Even concentrating long enough to have a simple conversation with a friend can seem like a mammoth task. And even if, were you to sit down and add up the figures, you found that you were getting seven or eight hours' sleep in total, it's the interruptions to the sleep that actually cause the problem.

Stress and emotional effects

A baby crying at night also causes stress. If this is your first baby, you are guaranteed to be doubly anxious about your baby's every whimper. So no wonder being woken by crying causes your heart to beat quicker, and your breath to shorten. At worst, this stress can cause physical ailments, such as constant headaches and ulcers.

A constant lack of sleep can send your emotions up the wall too. You might feel down and irritable, angry because you feel you're not coping, or even angry at the baby for keeping you awake. Remember, these are all normal emotions that you are quite entitled to feel. But don't take your anger out on your baby. She's an innocent who isn't aware of the effect her crying has on you, except that it brings you to her. Accept that parenting is a difficult and demanding job for every parent, and thankfully, there are a great many things you can do to help you feel better and to keep the effects of stress at bay.

• Eat a healthy diet, one that is full of fibre

and protein-rich foods to give you the energy to cope. Even if you are too tired to cook a five-course meal, there are lots of quick, snack-type foods that will fit the bill, for example, baked beans, baked potatoes, pasta, fruit and vegetables, and wholegrain breakfast cereals. Remember to drink plenty of water and fruit juice too, especially if you're breastfeeding baby.

- Don't expect too much of yourself. Ask for help, and accept help when it's offered.

- Exercise a little, each day if you can. Although you may be exhausted, keeping your body in shape will help you cope with the physical demands of looking after a baby. Even going for a brisk walk with the pram or running up the stairs, which you're probably climbing many times a day anyway, will serve the purpose.

- Remember you have needs too. Make some time for yourself, even if it's only half an hour relaxing in the bath or reading.

- Keep smiling and try to laugh about the situation because it *will* get better in time!

Your relationship

Interrupted sleep caused by a crying baby can make for strained relationships between couples. When they're feeling worn out through lack of sleep and the pressures of caring for a baby, it's normal for couples to blame each other when the baby cries, or to argue about whose turn it is to get up to see to the baby.

It's normal too for mums to feel resentful towards their partner because, although parent roles may have changed in recent years, mum is normally the one to bear the greatest burden of the baby's care. To help couples through the tiring times, mums need to make sure right from the start that dad feels included, and is an important person in caring for baby. Making sure he takes an active role will not only help to share the burden but is also very important in helping him to forge his own special relationship with the baby.

- Never blame each other. Care for your baby as a unit, sharing all the responsibilities and household chores as much as possible.

- However close you were before the birth, don't expect your partner to be able to read your mind. Let each other know if there is a problem and share your feelings.

- Make time for each other and talk about your day. Go to bed together, early if you can.

- Whenever possible, take in it turns to mind the baby during the day so that you can both have opportunities to catch up on your sleep.

Most importantly, try to maintain your sense of humour! Your baby's sleep patterns should become more predictable as the months go by, so things will improve.

CHAPTER 10

Where to get help

As a parent, you might experience times when nights of interrupted sleep and the time and effort spent in comforting a wakeful baby can just seem too much. Parenting can sometimes be a difficult job even for the most determined amongst us. Take heart in the fact that any of the problems you encounter in helping your baby to sleep through the night have already been and are continuing to be experienced by mums and dads everywhere. You might recognise your own thoughts on the subject in these statements from parents, all of which are about completely normal emotions and problems.

"I've heard so many different reports about what causes cot death. I want to make sure that my baby is safe, but if I don't know what causes it, how can I know if what I'm doing is right? It's making me so anxious that I'm going in to her all the time listening for her breathing, so I'm even more exhausted then I ever dreamed I would be."

"Lots of my friends have had good results with sleep training their babies. Even after six months, he (the baby) seems to be waking more than ever, so I'd like to give it a try too. But isn't it wrong to neglect your baby when he's crying? I don't know what to do for the best."

"My baby seems to sleep fine during the day but it's a different story at night. He'll fall asleep in my arms while I'm feeding him, then as soon as I put him down he's wide awake and crying."

Because all babies are different, there are no concrete instructions for ensuring that your baby will sleep through the night. In the majority of cases, the tips featured in this book will be all that are needed to cope with any problems you might have. The good news is that when you need further expert help, it's only a telephone call away. Try your health visitor, GP, midwife or local child health clinic for advice on what help is available to you. In addition, the support groups listed here have many years of experience in providing help and encouragement or just a listening ear to the parents of problem sleepers. So don't feel concerned about getting in touch. Their support is there for you whenever you need it.

Serene (incorporating the CRY-SIS Helpline)

London WC1N 3XX
Helpline 020 7404 5011
(8am-11pm daily)

Provides emotional support and practical advice to parents dealing with excessive crying, demanding behaviour and sleep problems. Callers are put in touch with local volunteers who have had similar experiences.

National Childbirth Trust (NCT)

Alexandra House, Oldham Terrace,
Acton, London W3 6NH
Telephone 020 8992 8637
Help, support and advice for mothers.

Parentline Plus

Highgate Studios,
53-79 Highgate Road,
Kentish Town,
London NW5 1TL
Telephone 0808 800 2222
Textphone (for speech and hearing impaired)
0800 783 6783
Website www.parentlineplus.org.uk
Incorporates the 'Parentline' freephone helpline which offers support and information for anyone in a parenting role.

The Foundation for the Study of Infant Deaths (FSID)

14 Halkin Street
London
SW1X 7DP
24-hour Helpline 020 7235 1721
For information and advice on sudden infant death and infant health.

NSPCC

NSPCC National Centre
42 Curtain Road
London EC2A 3NH
Website www.nspcc.org.uk

The National Society for the Prevention of Cruelty to Children (NSPCC) is the UK's leading charity specialising in child protection and the prevention of cruelty to children. It also operates the NSPCC Child Protection Helpline – a free, 24-hour service which provides counselling, information and advice to anyone concerned about a child at risk of abuse. The Helpline number is 0808 800 5000, Textphone 0800 056 0566.

CHAPTER 11

Things to remember

- All babies are different, so their sleep patterns will vary.

- Studies in the UK have shown that in babies up to the age of 12 months, 29% wake once or more every night and 26% need more than 30 minutes to fall asleep.

- Try to share the caring and night-time duties equally with your partner from the start so that both of you have times when you can catch up on sleep. Ask for help, and accept help when it's offered.

- Don't expect miracles at once. Generally, babies wake most in the night during their first few months when they need feeding more frequently. Most babies don't sleep through until at least six months.

- Start a bedtime routine with bath, feed and bed as soon as you feel able to do so. A routine *will* help, so persevere with it.

- Cot death or SIDS only affects a very few babies (one in every 800). You can minimise the risks very easily by ensuring a cigarette-smoke-free atmosphere for your baby, always putting baby down to sleep on his back, and by not overheating his bedroom.

- Keep smiling! The sleepless nights will lessen in time, and expert help is only on the other end of the telephone whenever you need it.

Use this page to record useful telephone numbers

_____

_____

_____

_____

_____

_____

_____

_____

_____

_____

_____

_____

_____

_____

We hope you enjoyed reading this book and would like to read other titles in the NSPCC range. If you have any difficulty finding other titles you can order them direct (p&p is free) from Egmont World Limited, P O Box 7, Manchester M19 2HD. Please make a cheque payable to Egmont World Limited and list the titles(s) you want to order on a separate piece of paper.

Please don't forget to include your address and postcode.

Thank you

… and remember every book purchased means another contribution towards the NSPCC cause.

NSPCC Child Care Guides   £2.99

First-time Parent,
by Faye Corlett   0 7498 4669 0

Understanding Your Baby,
by Eileen Hayes   0 7498 46704

Understanding Your Toddler,
by Eileen Hayes   0 7498 4671 2

Toddler Talk and Learning,
by Ken Adams   0 7498 4776 X

Sleeping Through the Night,
by Faye Corlett   0 7498 4775 1

Bullying,
by Sheila Dore   0 7498 4766 2

A Special Child in the Family,
by Mal Leicester   0 7498 4673 9

Being Different,
by Mal Leicester   0 7498 4765 4

Potty Training and Child Development,
by Faye Corlett 0 7498 4763 8

Changing Families,
by Sheila Dore 0 7498 4762 X

Positive Parenting,
by Eileen Hayes 0 7498 4674 7

Bedtimes and Mealtimes,
by Margaret Bamforth 0 7498 4672 0

NSPCC Learning Guides £2.99
by Nicola Morgan

Get Ready for School 0 7498 4492 2

Reading and Writing at School 0 7498 4491 4

NSPCC Happy Kids Story Books £2.99
by Michaela Morgan

Maya and the New Baby. 0 7498 4637 2

Spike and the Footy Shirt 0 7498 4636 4

Jordan and the Different Day 0 7498 4638 0

Jody and the Biscuit Bully 0 7498 4635 6

Emily and the Stranger 0 7498 4639 9

Happy Kids All Together Now 0 7498 4640 2

Notes